THE GOSPEL OF JOHN

BOOK 2   CHAPTERS 11-21

john

BOOK 2   CHAPTERS 11-21

11 DISCUSSIONS FOR GROUP BIBLE STUDY
MARILYN KUNZ &
CATHERINE SCHELL

TYNDALE HOUSE
PUBLISHERS, INC.
WHEATON, ILLINOIS

Bible verses quoted in this guide are taken from the
Revised Standard Version.

Fourth printing, February 1982
Library of Congress Catalog Card Number 78-64487
ISBN 0-8423-1896-8
Printed in the United States of America

contents

Introduction, John, Book 1 and Book 2

Book 1—John 1-10 (Twelve discussions)

Book 1 of this study guide covers the ministry of Jesus from the time of his baptism by John the Baptist, through periods of increasing conflict with the Jewish religious leaders in Jerusalem. Though the study is listed as having twelve discussions, many groups will need fourteen sessions for it, since two of the studies probably will take two sessions each.

This study is suitable for groups who already have studied *Mark* and *Acts* in the Neighborhood Bible Studies series, and for groups who are familiar with the Bible and are accustomed to discussion study. ·

Book 2—John 11-21 (Eleven discussions)

Book 2 of this study guide covers the events leading up to and including the Passion, death, and resurrection of Jesus Christ. If this book is studied as a unit by itself, it is especially appropriate for a pre-Easter Lenten series of small group discussions for churches. Also, it is suitable for outreach neighborhood Bible study groups to undertake after completing the Gospel of John, Book 1.

When to Study the Gospel of John

It has been the common practice of many Christians to encourage people beginning a study of the New Testament to start by reading the Gospel of John. However, if you intend to begin a *discussion* Bible study with people who are studying together for the first time, we strongly encourage you to start such a group in the Gospel of Mark, moving next to the Acts of the Apostles. Then your group will be ready to benefit from a study of the Gospel of John.

An adult studying the Bible for the first time will find the text of Mark's Gospel simpler to handle and easier to understand since it is shorter, more direct in style, using little symbolism. The Gospel of John is written on two levels. John recounts historical events, but he is also concerned with the deeper meaning of these events, and the significance of all that Jesus said and did. This double level is difficult for newcomers to Bible study to handle, and a beginning group will soon find themselves "in deep waters."

How to Use
This Discussion Guide

Sharing leadership—why and how

Each study guide in the Neighborhood Bible Study series is prepared with the intention that the ordinary adult group will by using this guide be able to rotate the leadership of the discussion. Those who are outgoing in personality are more likely to volunteer to lead first, but within a few weeks it should be possible for almost everyone to have the privilege of directing a discussion session. Everyone, including people who may not yet have committed themselves to Christ, should take a turn in leading by asking the questions from the study guide.

Reasons for this approach are:

(1) The discussion leader will prepare in greater depth than the average participant.

(2) The experience of leading a study stimulates a person to be a better participant in the discussions led by others.

(3) Members of the group which changes discussion leadership weekly tend to feel that the group belongs to everyone in it. It is not "Mr. or Mrs. Smith's Bible Study."

(4) The Christian who by reason of spiritual maturity and wider knowledge of the Bible is equipped to be a spiritual leader in the group is set free to *listen* to everyone in the group in a way that is not possible when leading the discussion. He (she) takes his regular turn in leading as it comes around, but if he leads the first study in a series he must guard against the temptation to bring in a great deal of outside knowledge and source material which would make others feel they could not possibly attempt to follow his example of leadership.

For study methods and discussion techniques refer to the first booklet in this series, *How to Start a Neighborhood Bible Study*, as well as to the following suggestions.

How to prepare to participate in a study using this guide

(1) Read through the designated chapter daily during the week. Use it in your daily time of meditation and prayer, asking God to teach you what he has for you in it.

(2) Take two or three of the guide questions each day and try to answer them from the passage. Use these questions as tools to dig deeper into the passage. In this way you can cover all the guide questions before the group discussion.

(3) Use the summary questions to tie together the whole chapter in your thinking.

(4) *As an alternative* to using this study in your daily quiet time, spend at least one hour in sustained study once during the week, using the above suggestions.

How to prepare to lead a study

(1) Follow the above suggestions on preparing to participate in a study. Pray for wisdom and the Holy Spirit's guidance.

(2) Familiarize yourself with the study guide questions until you can rephrase them in your own words if necessary, so you feel comfortable using them in the discussion.

(3) If you are familiar with the questions in the guide, you will be able to skip questions already answered by the group from discussion raised by another question. Try to get the movement of thought in the whole chapter so that you are able to be flexible in using the questions.

(4) Some of the studies will require two sessions. It is *not* recommended that you spend more than two sessions on one discussion. Each session should run from an hour to an hour and a half. Most of the discussions will require only one session, especially if everyone comes well-prepared.

(5) Pray for the ability to guide the discussion with love and understanding. Pray for the members of your group during the week preceding the study you are to lead.

How to lead a study

(1) Begin with a short prayer asking for God's help in the study. You may ask another member of the group to pray if you have asked him (her) ahead of time.

(2) Have the Bible portion read aloud by paragraphs (thought units), not verse by verse. It is not necessary for everyone to read aloud or for each to read an equal amount.

(3) Guide the group to discover what the passage says by asking the *discussion questions. Avoid going woodenly through the study using each and every question.* The group will often answer two or three questions in their answers to, and discussion of, one question. Omit those questions already answered. If you cannot discern the meaning of a question, don't use it, or else say to the group that you don't understand the question but they might. If they find it difficult, leave it and try simply to find the main point of the Bible paragraph.

(4) Use the suggestions from the section on *How to encourage everyone to participate.*

(5) Encourage everyone in the group to be honest in self-appraisal. If you are honest in your response to the Scripture, others will tend to be honest also.

(6) Allow time at the end of the discussion to answer the *summary questions* which help to tie the whole study together.

(7) The *afterthoughts* are primarily to stimulate personal reflection on what has been studied together.

(8) Bring the discussion to a close at the end of the time allotted. Close with a prayer relevant to what has been discussed.

How to encourage everyone to participate

(1) It is helpful to have several Bible translations available in the group. Encourage people to read aloud from these different translations as appropriate in the discussion. Of the many translations used in preparation of this study guide, particular references have been made by the following abbreviations: GNB—*Good News Bible;* NIV—*New International Ver-*

sion; RSV—*Revised Standard Version;* TLB—*The Living Bible.*

(2) Encourage discussion by asking several people to contribute answers to a question. "What do the rest of you think?" or "Is there anything else which could be added?" are ways of encouraging discussion.

(3) Be flexible and skip any questions which do not fit into the discussion as it progresses.

(4) Deal with irrelevant issues by suggesting that the purpose of your study is to discover what is *in the passage.* Suggest an informal chat about tangential or controversial issues after the regular study is dismissed.

(5) Receive all contributions warmly. Never bluntly reject what anyone says, even if you think the answer is incorrect. Instead ask in a friendly manner, "Where did you find that?" or "Is that actually what it says?" or "What do some of the rest of you think?" Allow the group to handle problems together.

(6) Be sure you don't talk too much as the leader. Redirect those questions which are asked you. A discussion should move in the form of an asterisk, back and forth between members, not in the form of a fan, with the discussion always coming back to the leader. The leader is to act as moderator. As members of a group get to know each other better, the discussion will move more freely, progressing from the fan to the asterisk pattern.

(7) Don't be afraid of pauses or long silences. People need time to think about the questions and the passage. Try not to answer your own question—either use an alternate question or move on to another area for discussion.

(8) Watch hesitant members for an indication by facial expression or body posture that they have something to say, and then give them an encouraging nod or speak their names.

(9) Discourage too talkative members from monopolizing the discussion by specifically directing questions to others. If necessary, speak privately to the over-talkative one about the need for discussion rather than lecture in the group, and enlist his aid in encouraging all to participate.

What rules make for an effective discussion?

(1) Everyone in the group should *read the Bible passage* and, if possible, use the study guide in thoughtful *study* of the passage *before* coming to the group meeting.

(2) *Stick to the Bible passage under discussion.* Discover all that you can from this section of John's Gospel. Try to limit cross-references to those suggested in the study guide so that everyone has the opportunity to study them ahead of time. The person new to the Bible will not be needlessly confused, and you will avoid the danger of taking portions out of context.

(3) *Avoid tangents.* Many different ideas will be brought to mind as you study each chapter of John. If an idea is not dealt with in any detail in a particular chapter, try not to let it occupy long discussion that week. Appoint a recorder in your group to make note of this and other such questions that arise from week to week. As your group studies on in the book of John, you may find some of these questions are dealt with in later chapters.

(4) Since the three-fold purpose of an inductive Bible study is to discover what the Bible portion says, what it means, and how it applies to you, your group should remember that *the Gospel of John is the authority for your study.* The aim of your group should be to discover what John is saying, to discover his message about Jesus.

If you don't like something that John says, be honest enough to admit that you don't like it. Do not rewrite the Bible to make it agree with your ideas. You may say that you do not agree with John or that you wish he had not said this, but don't try to make him say what he does not say. It is John's account that you are investigating. Let him state his own case about Jesus.

(5) *Apply to your own life what you discover in the study of John's Gospel.* Much of the vitality of any group Bible study depends upon honest sharing on the part of different members of the group. Discoveries made in Bible study should become guides for right action in life situations today.

John states that the intention of his book is *that you may believe that Jesus is the Christ, the Son of God, and that believing you may have life in his name* (20:31). As you study his account, you have the opportunity to face the implications for your life of Jesus' claims.

(6) *Let honesty with love be the attitude of your group toward one another.* Those who do not believe that Jesus is the Christ, the Son of God, should be able to voice their doubts and questions without feeling rejected or feeling that they should cover up their thinking. Those who do believe and are committed to Jesus as Lord and Savior should be free to share how this belief affects their lives (as appropriate to the section of John under discussion).

Introduction
to the Gospel of John

The Fourth Gospel, the Gospel according to John, differs in a number of ways from the other three accounts of Jesus' life. The records of Matthew, Mark, and Luke are called the Synoptic Gospels because they give the same general picture of the life of Jesus and contain so much common material that they can be conveniently studied together. A summary is given below in which the Synoptic Gospels and the Fourth Gospel are compared.

MATTHEW, MARK, LUKE	JOHN
They look at Jesus' teaching as it was given to the people of Galilee. They record no visits to Jerusalem or teaching given there except for Jesus' visit as a boy, and the last week of his life.	This Gospel is mainly concerned with Jesus' teaching in Jerusalem over a three-year period. It records only a few brief incidents in the life of Jesus outside Jerusalem.
Jesus' teaching is recorded in the form of short sayings and parables relating to scenes and people familiar to villagers and country folk.	No parables are recorded, though some short sayings are. Jesus' teaching is usually presented in the form of conversations with an individual or a group, or of long discourses either to the disciples or to *the Jews* (the section of the people very doubtful about the truth of his claims, or hostile to him).

Jesus' teaching deals mainly with the kingdom of heaven, its nature, the manner of its coming, and the conduct which will fit men to enter it.	Jesus' teaching often deals with the relationship between himself and God, and treats of themes such as life, light, truth and love.
Little is said about Jesus' teaching of individuals.	Several accounts of some length are given of Jesus' dealings with individuals (but these are still in compressed form, including only the outline of the conversation).
Jesus is presented as teaching with authority and making such claims upon his followers as would indicate his position as Messiah, but he says little about his person explicitly.	Jesus makes specific claims about who he is and what his relationship is with God.
Jesus' teaching usually is addressed to the ordinary country people of his day.	Jesus' discourses to *the Jews* are addressed to the educated class of the nation. They contain types of argument similar to those used in the schools of the Rabbis of that day.

Material within the Gospel of John indicates that its writer was a Jew of Palestine who was an eyewitness of most of the events presented, and an intimate associate of Jesus. Conservative scholars consider the writer to be the Apostle John, a view supported by the early Christian writers, Polycarp and Irenaeus. His purpose in writing (found in John 20:31) is to persuade his readers to personal belief in Jesus as the Christ, the Son of God. It is generally agreed that the book was written late in the first century, probably about A.D. 90 at Ephesus.

Discussion 1 / John 11:1-54

The Resurrection of Lazarus

Unlike Western culture which acknowledges death with little public manifestation of grief, Eastern cultures observe death with much noise. In Jesus' day it was customary to hire mourners to console the bereaved with loud wailings and much weeping. Since the climate necessitated burial almost immediately after death, the formal grieving continued a number of days after the burial.

John 11:1-16

1. On the map on page 55, locate Bethany and the place where Jesus was (10:40).

2. What situation has arisen in Bethany? Why do Mary and Martha send for Jesus?

3. Put yourself in the place of the sisters and Lazarus after Jesus has been sent for. What thoughts and feelings do you experience?

4. What is Jesus' reaction when he hears of Lazarus' illness? What is the purpose of this illness? See also 9:2, 3. Consider the possibility of some illness today being for this same purpose.

5. In the light of Jesus' relationship to the three, how do you account for his remaining where he was for two days? What would the sisters expect him to do? Why are we so often in conflict with God's timing?

Note—If it took the messenger a day to get to Jesus and it took Jesus a day to get to Bethany, with Jesus delaying two days and Lazarus having been in the grave four days when

Jesus arrived, it may be assumed that Lazarus was already dead when the message reached Jesus.

6. Why do the disciples object to going to Judea? See also John 8:58, 59; 10:31, 39. How does Jesus answer his disciples' objection? Put his answer into your own words if you can.

7. When Jesus states his purpose for going to Bethany (verse 11), how do his disciples misunderstand him? Why is Jesus glad he was not there when Lazarus died? What is Jesus' intention for his disciples in this matter?

8. What attitude does Thomas express?

John 11:17-27

9. Describe the situation in the home at Bethany. Remember the atmosphere which prevailed at the last funeral which you attended.

10. Picture the scene on the road as Martha approaches Jesus. What would be Martha's feelings? What might be the disciples' reactions?

11. Have the brief exchange between Martha and Jesus read aloud as a dialogue. Compare the statements of fact made by Jesus and Martha. What is Martha's expectation? Jesus' declaration?

12. What is Jesus concerned that Martha believe? Why? How does Jesus direct Martha's thinking from the future to the present? How does Martha's final declaration in this section fall short of what Jesus is saying?

13. Make a list of all the great *I am* declarations which Jesus has made in the Gospel of John thus far. (Note 4:25, 26; 6:35; 8:12; 10:7, 11; 11:25.)

John 11:28-44

14. Contrast Mary's meeting with Jesus to Martha's. What new sights and sounds are there? The fact that both women use the same words as they greet Jesus indicates that it is probably something which they have said over and over to each other. What difference may there be in the way in which they say it because of their different personalities?

15. What insight do you get into Jesus' own attitude and feelings? How do you account for the fact that in verse 15 he is *glad* and in verse 35 he *weeps?* Why does Jesus weep since he knows he is going to raise Lazarus?

16. How do the two different reactions from the people epitomize the reactions of people today? Does verse 37 express faith or doubt?

17. Why does Martha object to Jesus' command? What does this reveal about her understanding of her earlier conversation with him?

18. Compare Jesus' statement in 11:40 to 10:37, 38; 7:16, 17; 6:69; 3:18. What spiritual principle do these verses all emphasize?

19. How does Jesus now clarify for Martha what he said to her in verse 25? Note what he had told the disciples in verse 4.

20. Why does Jesus pray? In order that Lazarus might be released, what three commands must be obeyed? Who must obey?

21. What authority and what relationship does Jesus reveal?

22. What range of emotions do you think Mary and Martha experience in verses 38-44?

John 11:45-54

23. How do the two reactions of the Jews parallel the reactions of people today?

24. What are the results of this incident?

SUMMARY

1. Picture this event in a contemporary setting. How do you feel as a witness to this miracle? What will you always remember? How does this change your attitude toward death?

2. Since you may decide to respond as those in verses 37 and 46, or as those in verses 36 and 45, which do you choose? What are you going to do about your choice?

3. All of us sometime will experience the pangs of bereavement, when we will think that only the return of that

person could fill the emptiness or heal the bitter grief. Remember that the words of Jesus in verses 25, 26 are not merely words but something he is, something he has proved. The only condition is our belief.

AFTERTHOUGHTS

Lazarus, did you live the rest of your life differently because of the resurrection you experienced? Did you value the gift of life in a deeper way than we do? Remembering your experience, I want to value life more fully, live more thankfully each day.

Discussion 2 / John 11:55—12:50

Those Who Acclaim Jesus

After the conversations which Jesus held in the Temple in September or October during the Feast of Tabernacles (7:14—8:59), and in December during the Feast of the Dedication (10:22-39), he kept away from Jerusalem (10:40; 11:54) until the time of Passover in early spring. With the exception of his brief trip to Bethany, two miles from Jerusalem, for the raising of Lazarus, Jesus had not taught nor had crowds followed him in Jerusalem for a period of about three months.

John 11:55—12:8

1. If you were directing a film of this section, what elements would you highlight? How?
2. Describe the atmosphere in 12:1-8. Contrast Mary's attitude and actions toward Jesus and her motives with those of Judas. How does Jesus interpret the incident?

John 12:9-19

3. It is apparent that there were actually two crowds, the group which had gone to Bethany to find Jesus and traveled with him to Jerusalem, and the group in Jerusalem who went out to meet him. What motivates both these groups? With what significance does the author of this Gospel clothe their actions?
4. How do the Pharisees interpret this incident? What

fears and what plans do they have (11:47, 48, 53, 57; 12:10, 11, 19)? Why is Lazarus in danger?

John 12:20-36a

5. These Greeks are Gentile converts to Judaism. How does Jesus interpret their request? What is the full meaning of *the hour* for him? What is the significance of the illustration he uses?

6. What does it mean to "love your life"? What does it mean to "hate your life"? Give a present-day example of each. Jesus himself set an example of what it is to hate one's life. How can you truly follow him in this?

7. How is verse 32 an answer to the Greeks' request to *see* Jesus? Why is seeing not enough? What does Jesus promise those who serve and follow him?

8. How is the prayer Jesus prays the opposite of the one which he rejects? Why does he reject the first prayer? What insight do you get into Jesus' mood?

9. What are the two reactions from the crowd to the voice from heaven? Compare these reactions with the ones in 11:45, 46; 11:36, 37; and 10:20, 21. Do you prefer natural or supernatural explanations?

10. In what three ways does Jesus describe his death in verses 31, 32? What claim does he make which would include the Greeks?

11. What troubles the crowd which has just welcomed him with great acclaim? Why are his statements inconsistent with their understanding?

12. Why are Jesus' declarations particularly disconcerting to the crowds who have come up for the festivities at Jerusalem? (What incident had spurred them to give him a victory parade?)

13. This is Jesus' last recorded interview with the people in the Gospel of John. Notice that only shortly after they eagerly proclaimed him as King, the last tragic question they ask Jesus is, *Who is this Son of man?* or "Who are you?" They want to talk about raising the dead and political deliverance, and Jesus talks about crucifixion.

14. What is Jesus' final warning to them in verses 35, 36?

What two responses does he urge from them concerning the light? What reasons does he give for doing these two things? Rephrase this admonition in your own words without using the metaphor of light and darkness.

John 12:36b-43

15. What is the author's concluding estimate of the crowd's response to Jesus? What opportunity have they had? How do they fail? Why?

16. While the Jews are concerned about the fulfillment of the law or prophecy in verse 34, how does the author see that prophecy is being fulfilled? (See Isaiah 53:1, 6, 10.)

17. What prevented some (verses 42, 43) from acting on Jesus' admonition? How would you say that this prevents some from coming to the Lord Jesus today?

John 12:44-50

18. What does Jesus say is involved in a relationship to him? What verbs suggest the possible responses to Jesus and the results?

19. If you had only these words of Jesus, what would you know about him? About his mission?

SUMMARY

1. Observe the references to Lazarus in 12:1, 2, 9-11, 17-19. What are the various results of the raising of Lazarus?

2. Describe to a friend what you saw, what you heard, and what you felt as one of the crowd from Bethany, as one of the crowd in Jerusalem who went out to meet Jesus, as one of the Greeks, as one of the Pharisees, as one of the disciples. (Ask different members of the group to take different parts.)

3. Discuss the danger of *seeing,* yet not *believing* (verse 37), and the danger of *believing* and yet not *confessing* or committing (verse 42).

4. There may be some today who follow along in the

crowd because they enjoy waving palm branches and are eager to partake of any fringe benefits they can get. Review the words of Jesus in this study to those who would acclaim him. Consider prayerfully the meaning of verses 25, 26, substituting your own name for *any one*.

AFTERTHOUGHTS

Philip, why is it we so often respond as you did when the Greeks wanted to see Jesus? We feel inadequate and unsure. Jesus directs us to the cross as the way of "seeing him."

Discussion 3 / John 13

Status Seekers

This chapter is the beginning of Jesus' last conversation with his disciples before his crucifixion. This section through chapter 16 is referred to as the upper room discourse since it forms the last pre-resurrection teachings of Jesus to his disciples. Chapter 17 is his great high-priestly prayer. In order to understand the attitude which prevails among the disciples at the beginning of these talks, read Matthew 20:20-28 and Luke 22:24-27. The disciples have become concerned about position and relative greatness among themselves. They have become status seekers. (Foot-washing, a function of the servants in a household, was necessary because of the open sandal-like footwear and the unpaved dusty roads.)

John 13:1-20

1. How should the approaching Passover have affected the mood of the supper? What, however, are the disciples evidently thinking about? (See Matthew 20:20-28 and Luke 22:24-27.)

2. What does Jesus *know?* (verses 1, 3, 11). Contrast the work of Jesus and the work of the devil in verses 1, 2.

3. If you were one of the disciples, how would you feel when Jesus gets up and takes the towel and basin? Who washes Jesus' feet?

4. Ask two people to read aloud to the group the exchange between Jesus and Peter. How would you characterize Peter's attitude at first?

5. How does Jesus handle Peter's refusal? Think about

the fact that Jesus does not violate Peter's will, and compare him with world leaders and rulers who impose their own wills by force on their followers.

6. Why do you think the Lord makes his purposes dependent upon our acquiescence?

7. What is Jesus' teaching about cleansing? How can he cleanse as no one else can?

8. Through this object lesson what is Jesus seeking to teach his disciples? How should this answer their dispute about greatness?

9. How can a status seeker be happy or blessed? In what area are you concerned about status?

10. What claim is Jesus making concerning himself and the Old Testament Scripture? (Compare verse 18 and Psalm 41:9.)

11. What does *I am he* (verse 19) mean? (See also John 8:24, 28.)

12. Compare verse 20 with John 12:44, 45. What addition does Jesus make in verse 20?

John 13:21-30

13. Trace throughout this chapter Jesus' awareness of his forthcoming betrayal. How does the section 21-30 fulfill the prophecy in verse 18? (To give a morsel of bread dipped in wine to anyone was a mark of special honor and good will, and in this instance it was Jesus' last appeal to Judas.)

14. How do the disciples react to Jesus' statement that one of them will betray him? In what way are they still concerned with their personal status? What inner conflicts may each have? How do they acknowledge that Jesus knows them better than they know themselves?

15. Try to imagine the conflicting thoughts in Judas' heart, and the emotions of the Lord Jesus throughout the supper. (For further understanding of Judas see John 12:1-6.)

16. How do the disciples account for Judas' departure? Why don't they catch on to the fact that Jesus has indicated that Judas will betray him? What do you think they would do if they realized it?

17. What does Jesus teach here about his glorification? Compare verses 31, 32 with John 12:23, 24, 31-33.

18. Now that Judas has gone out and the end is near, notice how tenderly Jesus addresses the disciples. For what is he preparing them?

19. Why is his new commandment to them so vital at this point? What effect will obedience to it have?

20. Have the conversation in verses 36-38 read aloud for the group. What is Peter concerned about? What may he still be trying to establish?

21. What two things does Jesus say about Peter? How does his estimate of Peter differ from Peter's estimate of himself?

SUMMARY

1. What needs and weaknesses do the disciples have?

2. At the first Passover the death of the innocent was God's instrument for deliverance. At this Passover how will God's great deliverance be accomplished?

3. What practical applications can you make to your own life of what this passage teaches about status, love, and self-knowledge?

4. From observing Jesus' dealings with his status-seeking disciples here, what do you learn about how to treat someone who is always trying to prove his position of greatness? How do you react to someone who continually makes unreasonable demands upon you?

AFTERTHOUGHTS

Judas, what was it that caused you to rush out into the night? Was it frustration because Jesus washed the disciples' feet? Your feet? What were you thinking when Jesus gave you the favored morsel? How terrifying to reject the Lord's grace and mercy!

Review Judas :

verse :

Discussion 4 / John 14

The Troubled

After washing his disciples' feet at supper, Jesus has predicted his betrayal by one of the twelve and warned Peter that he will soon deny Jesus. The words of comfort in this chapter are spoken after Judas has left the room. In the long conversation that follows, Jesus concentrates on the needs of his disciples.

John 14:1-7

1. See John 13:21, 33, 38 for reasons the disciples have to be troubled and upset. What does Jesus ask them to do instead of worrying?

2. What two things will Jesus do when he leaves them? What new information does he give his disciples here? What is Jesus' ultimate purpose in leaving them now?

3. What is Thomas' reaction to Jesus' statement that they know the way to the place where Jesus is going? From Jesus' statement in verse 6, where is he going?

4. Put Jesus' four claims in verse 6 into your own words.

5. What additional claim does Jesus make in verse 7? How does his claim answer the statement we sometimes hear today, "Jesus was a good man but he never claimed to be God"?

John 14:8-14

6. Try to put yourself in Philip's place. What motivates your request and what do you mean by it? How would you

respond then to the questions Jesus asks in verses 9, 10? What answer is Jesus giving to Philip's questions?

7. What should the words and the works of Jesus reveal (verses 10, 11)? Compare 1:14, 18.

8. Having established his claims concerning his relationship to the Father, what other relationship does Jesus discuss (verses 12-14)? What promises does he make? Why will the requests of Jesus' followers be answered? What does it mean to ask in Jesus' name?

John 14:15-24

9. What theme does Jesus emphasize throughout this section (verses 15, 21, 23, 24)? What is the test of one's love for the Lord? What great benefits come to the one who obeys Jesus' teaching?

10. Find at least six things Jesus says about the Counselor or Helper (verses 16, 17). What will this Counselor do for them that Jesus now can not?

11. What event and what consequent change in the disciples does Jesus foretell (verses 18-21)? Compare Mark 9:31; 10:34; 14:28.

12. Why will Jesus reveal himself to those who love him and not to the world?

John 14:25-31

13. List at least four things revealed about the Holy Spirit. How do his actions fit his name of Counselor or Helper?

14. What great gift does Jesus leave his disciples? What reasons does he give his disciples not to be afraid or troubled? What is Jesus' intention in telling them all this now?

15. What do verses 30, 31 indicate about the death of Jesus?

SUMMARY

1. Look again at the requests made by the three disciples

in verses 5, 8, 22. Summarize Jesus' answers to their questions in three or four sentences.

2. How do the other promises Jesus made to his disciples throughout this chapter relate to his gift of peace (verse 27)?

3. What have you learned from this chapter about the Holy Spirit?

4. In later years as one of Jesus' disciples, what would you remember as the most important thing Jesus told you that night? Why?

AFTERTHOUGHTS

Philip, did you forget what the Greeks had asked for (12:31)? You might not have needed to make your request in 14:8 if you had understood Jesus' answer for the Greeks. Do we, too, still ask for things or experiences we "need" to increase our faith and understanding?

Discussion 5 / John 15

Fruit-bearing Branches

Because chapter 14 ends with Jesus' words, *Rise, let us go hence* (RSV), some scholars would place chapters 15 and 16 before 14, seeing Jesus' exhortation in 14:31 as the conclusion of his teaching in the upper room. If the Gospel account is taken as it stands, however, chapters 15 and 16 must have been spoken as Jesus and his disciples walked to the garden across the Kidron valley (18:1).

In the Old Testament the nation of Israel is seen as a grape vine or a vineyard that God planted, from which he expected fruit. (See Isaiah 5:1-7; Psalm 80:8-16.)

John 15:1-11

1. In the light of the Old Testament picture of Israel as God's vine, what do you think that Jesus means by his declaration, *I am the true vine?*

2. What relationship does Jesus picture between himself and his disciples? What is the goal or purpose of this relationship? How does the Father intervene to make sure that the goal is accomplished?

3. What two things are expected of the branches? What has already happened to them? Compare verse 3 with 6:63.

4. Share your understanding of what it means to abide (remain) in Jesus Christ and to have Jesus Christ abide in you (verse 5). What is Jesus' explanation of how to abide in him (verses 7, 10)?

5. What warning and what promises are introduced by the three *if* clauses in verses 6, 7, 10? According to verses 8, 11, what will be the results of understanding and obeying Jesus' commands?

6. What kind of fruit had Jesus been looking for from his disciples earlier that evening? See 13:14-17.

John 15:12-17

7. What example has been set for what Jesus is calling his disciples to do? What is the ultimate test of love?

8. Why do you think Jesus commands his disciples to love one another, rather than asking them to love him? How can they prove their love for him? To what new relationship does Jesus introduce them? How does it differ from the old?

9. Why do you think Jesus addresses his commands and promises to the disciples as a group, rather than as individuals? Who chose whom? For what purpose? What special provision is made for them to carry out their task?

10. Compare verse 17 with Romans 12:4, 5, 10. What interrelationship makes Jesus' command necessary not only to his disciples and the Christians of the early Church, but to us today? Give contemporary examples of Christians obeying this command.

John 15:18-21

11. What do the four *if* clauses (verses 18-20) prepare Jesus' disciples to expect? Why does identification with Jesus bring separation from the world?

12. From this section give at least four reasons why the world *hates* the followers of Jesus. How is this hatred expressed? See also Matthew 10:16-22; 1 Peter 4:14.

13. What are the characteristics of *the world* in our day from which Christians should be different? What positive actions should a Christian today take which may bring rejection from *the world?* Be specific.

John 15:22-27

14. In the parallel statements in verses 22, 24, what are the actions of Jesus and the consequences of these actions? Compare 9:39-41.

15. From this section, how would you describe what sin is? What do verses 23, 24b add to your understanding of what sin basically is? Why is it not possible to reject Jesus and still love the Father?

16. In our society today there are few people who would actually say that they *hate* Jesus. Nevertheless, how are hatred and rejection of Jesus expressed today?

17. Compare verse 25 (which is a quotation from Psalm 35:19; 69:4) with John 12:37-41; 13:11, 18. What reasons are there for the people to love Jesus rather than to hate him from the things he has said and done thus far in John's Gospel?

18. What does 15:26 add to what Jesus has already told his disciples about the Holy Spirit in 14:16, 17, 26? Comparing 14:26 and 15:26, what do you discover about the coming of the Holy Spirit?

19. What responsibility do Jesus' disciples share with the Holy Spirit? Why? How would you define *bear witness* or *testify?* What do you think is the nature of an appropriate Christian witness today?

SUMMARY

1. From this chapter what do you learn about the relationship between: Jesus and the Father, Jesus and his disciples, Jesus and the world, the disciples and one another, the disciples and the world?

2. What, do you think, are the three major things Jesus is trying to teach his disciples in this chapter?

AFTERTHOUGHTS

Lord, the disciples with all their faults and weaknesses did speak about you to the world of their day. Now it is our turn, our responsibility. Help us to be your witnesses.

Discussion 6 / John 16

The Father, the Son, and the Spirit

Chapters 13-17 should be considered as a unit since they are the final instructions Jesus leaves with his disciples on the night of his arrest. The traumatic events described in chapter 18 and following would only increase the impact of these instructions on their minds and hearts. Review briefly the major things you remember from chapters 13, 14, 15 before you discuss chapter 16.

John 16:1-4

1. For what troubles is Jesus preparing his disciples? From what source may they expect trouble and what is the extent of their danger? What will these actions toward Jesus' followers reveal about the people who do them?

2. What is Jesus' intention in giving his disciples this advance warning? Read verse 1 in several translations including NIV, RSV, GNB, TLB.

3. Compare 16:4 with 13:33, 36; 14:3, 25, 28. To what change is Jesus alerting his disciples?

John 16:5-15

4. What reactions does Jesus observe in his disciples? Imagining yourself as one of the disciples, describe your emotions at what you have been hearing this evening. Yet why is it to your advantage that Jesus leave?

5. How does Jesus try to allay the disciples' fears and sorrow (verses 7-11)? Add 16:7 to what they already have been told about the Spirit in 14:26; 15:26.

6. What will the Counselor do in relation to the world? Through whom? (See 15:26, 27.)

7. On what basis will the world be proved wrong (convicted) about *sin?* Compare verse 9 with 15:22, 24. See also the end of Peter's first sermon after the resurrection, Acts 2:36, 37.

8. Concerning *righteousness* (verse 10), see Acts 3:14, 15. Concerning *judgment* (verse 11), see John 12:31, 32.

9. Describe all that the Spirit will do for Jesus' disciples (verses 13-15). What will the Spirit *not* do? To what one end is the Spirit's activity directed?

10. From this section, what do you know about the Trinity? What standard do these verses give you for checking whether something said or taught today is truly from the Holy Spirit?

John 16:16-24

11. What is the disciples' reaction to what Jesus tells them about the immediate future? List the different points Jesus makes in his answer (verses 20-24).

12. How do a woman's emotions in childbirth illustrate what the disciples will soon experience?

13. What does Jesus emphasize about the qualities of the joy they will experience? What connection does this joy have with Jesus' promises here about prayer?

14. What does it mean to *ask in my* (Jesus') *name?*

John 16:25-33

15. Note the references to time in verses 24-26. What changes will time bring in the disciples' situation? What new pattern for prayer will be established? See also Acts 3:6.

16. Why can the disciples be certain of the Father's love? Could this be said about you?

17. Where has Jesus come from and where is he going? What is the disciples' response to this plain statement? What levels of belief and understanding have you experienced in your Christian life? At each level, why do we tend to think we have reached the ultimate in understanding?

18. Why does Jesus question the disciples' declaration? What firm confidence does Jesus have (verses 32, 33)? Compare verse 33 with 14:27. From these verses how would you advise a person who is looking for "peace"?

SUMMARY

1. Trace through this chapter the reasons Jesus gives his disciples as to why he tells, or does not tell, them certain things. What motivates his teaching in this chapter?

2. What evidence do you see of the disciples' need for the Holy Spirit when Jesus returns to the Father? How would you characterize their belief?

3. Contrast the work of the Holy Spirit in relation to *the world* with his ministry to those who love Jesus.

AFTERTHOUGHTS

Oh, dear disciples, how we see ourselves in your self-confidence and in your weakness! The way you were is both a warning and a challenge to us.

Discussion 7 / John 17

Jesus' Prayer

This chapter is unique because it gives the reader insight into the heart and mind of Jesus during the most trying hours of his life. Jesus no longer is speaking to his disciples as in the previous two chapters. Here he talks to his Father. From this prayer the disciples will learn Jesus' concerns for himself, for them, and for all believers. This is the last time the disciples are alone with Jesus before his death.

John 17:1-5

1. What *time* or *hour* has come? What is the meaning of this term as it is used throughout the Gospel of John? Note 2:4; 7:30; 8:20; 12:23, 27; 13:1.

2. For whom does Jesus pray? What two requests does he make?

3. How has Jesus glorified the Father? Compare verse 4; 1:14, 17, 18.

4. How does Jesus define *eternal life?* How is it obtained? List in your own words what has already been said about eternal life in 3:14, 15; 5:39, 40; 6:54, 68; 10:27, 28; 12:25. What does each reference add to your understanding of what eternal life is and how one gets it?

5. How will the Father glorify the Son? Compare verses 1, 5 with 1:1-4; Philippians 2:5-11.

John 17:6-19

6. In this section, for whom does Jesus pray? What has he done for them? What has been their response?

7. Since Jesus is leaving his disciples, what two major requests does he make of the Father?

8. The term *Holy Father* (verse 11) appears nowhere else in the Gospels. What connection do you see between this name and the particular requests Jesus makes in verses 11, 12, 15-19?

9. What dangers to Jesus' disciples are indicated by his words in verses 11, 12, 14, 15? What has Jesus done for his disciples while he has been with them?

10. Note Jesus' emphasis on the *word* and *truth* of God in his prayer (verses 6, 8, 14, 17). What knowledge comes from a positive response to the word of truth (verses 7, 8b)? What other results are there (verses 14, 15, 17)?

11. Compare verses 18, 19 with verse 8. How would you diagram the flow of action described here? What tremendous responsibility now belongs to the disciples?

John 17:20-23

12. Jesus enlarges the scope of his prayer. For whom and for what does he now pray? For what ultimate purpose?

13. What two things will the world *know* from the unity of Christian believers?

14. What triangular unity of relationships is described here?

John 17:24-26

15. What new petition does Jesus make for those who will love him? Compare verse 24, verse 5, and 1:1-3.

16. Note the name by which Jesus addresses the Father (verse 25). Who knows the Father and who does not?

17. What picture do these verses give of the position Jesus occupies between the Father and all those who believe in Jesus? See also 1 Timothy 2:5, 6.

18. By what work will Jesus continue to make the Father known to his disciples (verse 26)? Why?

SUMMARY

1. What qualities should characterize all of Jesus' followers as they live in the world?

2. Summarize briefly the requests Jesus made for himself, for his disciples, and for those who would believe through their message.

3. What insight does Jesus' prayer give you into his relationship with his Father? Into his relationship with his disciples?

AFTERTHOUGHTS

I never realized I was so specifically mentioned in the Bible, but surely in verse 20 Jesus is praying for me!

[Handwritten notes:]

PRAYER.

1. Glorify his name . { Prayers to Jesus prayers.

   ". . ." me.

2. Disciples — prayed for Sanctification praying together with God the Father

3. Glorification given to disciples

   Love / in me / in them:

   thing

   Prays Jesus.

   May love through knowledge of you . God .

Discussion 8 / John 18

Jesus' Captors, an Accuser, an Appeaser

The garden referred to in 18:1 is Gethsemane, and the Gospel of John does not record the Lord's prayer of agony described in the other Gospels. Although Annas is no longer the high priest, having been deposed a number of years previously by a former Roman governor, he is still very influential and in 18:19, 22 is referred to as the "high priest," much as ex-Presidents retain the title of "Mr. President." Nevertheless, the trial of Jesus before Annas was highly irregular and his scourging by the Romans before sentencing was not only irregular, but illegal according to Roman law and justice.

John 18:1-11

1. Picture the scene. What has this place been for Jesus and his disciples? Describe what you see and hear and feel as one of the disciples. If you were one of the soldiers, what sights and sounds would you particularly notice?

2. Why does Jesus ask, *Whom do you seek?* How can you account for the response of the soldiers? What things have they possibly heard about Jesus?

3. With what phrase does Jesus voluntarily present himself to them? (Compare John 8:24, 28; 13:19.) What is his attitude toward the disciples at this point?

4. How does Jesus interpret the situation to Peter?

5. Considering the conduct of Jesus and his captors, what impression do you get as to who is actually in command of the situation?

6. Relate in your own words, as one of the soldiers to his family later, the events of the night as they impressed you.

John 18:12-18

7. If you were asked to play the part of Peter in a film of this incident, what demeanor, movements, tone of voice, and inflections would you use to convey Peter's thoughts and feelings during these events?

8. What sort of situation do you find comparably threatening if you are pointed out as a Christian? Why?

John 18:19-24

9. What areas are covered by Annas' questioning? Why do you think Annas evidently avoids any question about the identity of Jesus, when this question was asked frequently by the crowds?

10. What claims does Jesus make concerning his teaching?

11. What responsibility is laid upon Annas and the officer by Jesus' response to the blow?

12. What conclusion does Annas seem to come to in sending Jesus to Caiaphas?

13. Concerning Caiaphas, compare verses 13, 14 with 11:47-53. From the council meeting following the resurrection of Lazarus in chapter 11, what does Caiaphas already know about Jesus when Jesus is brought before him? What has the high priest already decided?

John 18:25-27

14. During Jesus' interrogation by Annas, what is happening to Peter in the courtyard? Why would Peter come this far into the high priest's residence? Why, then, do you think that Peter reacts as he does when questioned twice by different people in the courtyard about his relationship to Jesus?

15. Compare verse 27 with 13:37, 38. Imagine Peter's consternation when he hears the cock crow. See also Mark 14:72.

16. What information does Pilate gather through his conversation with the Jews in verses 28-32?

17. Have the interview in verses 33-38 read as a dialogue to the group. What does Pilate's first question to Jesus indicate? Why does Jesus ask Pilate about the source of his information?

18. What does Jesus make clear about the nature of his kingship? What does he indicate about his purpose? What is the ground of Jesus' appeal to this Roman governor?

19. What conclusion does Pilate come to in the interview? What is his response to truth? How would you characterize a person who makes such a response today?

20. Although Pilate has concluded that Jesus claims to be a king, he evidently accepts Jesus' word that his kingship is not that of an insurrectionist. What does Pilate tell the Jews about his findings?

21. What attempt does Pilate make to get himself and Jesus out of this situation? What legal mistake does he make in offering to release an innocent man as an act of clemency? What seem to be Pilate's motives?

22. Compare verse 40 with Mark 15:6-11. What motives lie behind the Jews' request for the release of Barabbas?

23. See also verse 28. What is so ironic in the Jews' attitudes in this whole situation?

SUMMARY

1. What attitude and confidence does Jesus reveal in each of the three incidents—before his captors in the garden, before his accusers, and before Pilate the appeaser?

2. Each of the men who confront Jesus in this chapter has a heart and mind closed to him because of commitment to other authorities and ambitions. What authorities and ambitions rival Jesus Christ in your heart? How can you become fully committed to Christ as Lord in your life?

AFTERTHOUGHTS

Annas, what an ugly scene of usurped authority, improper procedures, frustration, and anger! What a sad warning you are to all in positions of religious responsibilities.

Discussion 9 / John 19

Jesus' Crucifixion and Burial

After his betrayal by Judas in the garden, Jesus has been brought before Annas, former high priest, and Caiaphas, the present high priest, and finally before Pilate, the Roman governor. Meanwhile Peter, waiting in the courtyard, has denied being one of Jesus' disciples. Pilate, convinced of Jesus' innocence, wants to release Jesus, but the Jews object. All of these events have taken place in the night hours following the Passover meal Jesus ate with his disciples.

John 19:1-16

1. Why would Pilate have Jesus whipped when he has just stated that he finds him innocent? Describe the struggle taking place in verses 4-7. Why do Pilate's attempts seem to backfire? What does each party want?

2. How do verses 4-7 highlight both the humanity and the deity of Jesus? What issue is clarified in verse 7? Why would the Jews' charge against Jesus make Pilate *more afraid?*

3. What impact have Pilate's judicial rulings in verses 4, 6 had? Why?

4. From verse 8 and following, as Jesus and Pilate face each other costumed in robes of authority, whose robes seem a mockery? Why? With what emotion, do you think, does Pilate ask his question (verse 9)?

5. When he gets no answer, how does Pilate react? What does this reveal about him? What is Jesus' answer to Pilate's threat?

6. Reread 18:29-31, 38-40; 19:4-7. What turning point do you see in Pilate's personal struggle (verse 12)? What power-

ful argument do the Jews use here to convince Pilate? On what consideration does Pilate base his final decision and action?

7. How does Pilate's question in 18:38 forecast the outcome described in 19:12-16? Why could 18:29—19:16 be called Pilate's trial?

8. Describe the last moments of Jesus' trial, which ends about noon *(the sixth hour)*. What terrible irony do you see in the exchange between Pilate and the Jews?

John 19:17-37

9. Describe the scene at Jesus' crucifixion and the sequence of events.

10. What further reason do the Jewish leaders find for conflict with Pilate? Compare this with Pilate's earlier concern with Jesus' identity (18:33, 37, 39). Who wins this argument?

11. What three incidents does John describe as fulfilling Old Testament prophecies about the Messiah? What various motivations do you see for the actions here? What reasons, if any, are given for these actions?

Old Testament references to look at are: Psalm 22:18; 69:21; 34:20; Numbers 9:12; Zechariah 12:10.

12. Contrast the four soldiers and the women at the cross in terms of mood and motive. Notice how the basic elements of clothing, shelter, and thirst are pictured in these moments of infinite significance for all humanity. How does Jesus care for his mother's need?

John 19:38-42

13. What happens now to involve Pilate with Jesus for the third time since he handed him over to the Jews to be crucified? Who are Joseph and Nicodemus? (See also Mark 15:43; Luke 23:50-53; John 3:1-10; 7:45-52.)

14. Compare verses 41, 42 with Matthew 27:59, 60. What do Nicodemus' provision of the great amount of spices (very costly) and Joseph's provision of his own tomb reveal about their attitudes toward Jesus? Considering the attitudes of most

47

of the council members, what risks are Nicodemus and Joseph taking? What do you imagine their conversation may include as they go about their work of burial?

SUMMARY

1. When you consider that all the events described in chapters 13-19 take place within only twenty-four hours, what does this indicate about the author's evaluation of the significance of these events?

2. What irregularities do you note in the trial of Jesus before Pilate (18:28—19:16)? Yet noting 18:11, 36 and 19:11, what is Jesus' attitude toward his arrest and trial?

3. What different things contributed to Jesus' sufferings in this chapter?

4. As you studied chapter 19, what was most impressive to you?

AFTERTHOUGHTS

Pilate, how much you represent "everyman" under pressure with an investment to protect. Your rejection of pressure in verse 22 comes too late to change you.

Discussion 10 / John 20

Resurrection!

Among those standing at the cross during Jesus' final hours was Mary of Magdala. When Joseph of Arimathea and Nicodemus prepared Jesus' body for burial, placed it in the garden tomb, and rolled a large stone in front of the entrance, Mary of Magdala was one of the women watching. (See Matthew 27:59-61; Mark 15:47; Luke 23:55, 56.) With the intervening Sabbath and its restrictions on activity, early Sunday morning would be the first opportunity any of the disciples and friends of Jesus would have to come to the tomb again.

John 20:1-18

1. What is Mary of Magdala's first reaction when she discovers the stone has been removed from the tomb? What does she assume has happened?

2. As Peter and *the other disciple* (thought to be John) run toward the tomb, what ideas must be going through their minds? What worse thing could possibly happen than has already happened?

3. Describe the sequence of events when the two disciples reach the tomb. What do they observe about the burial clothes? Who believes, and what?

4. Why are they unprepared for this event (Luke 24:25, 26, 45, 46)? What are the possible reasons that the two disciples return home at this point?

5. Trace Mary's movements in verses 1-11. If the other apostle (John) was hesitant to go into the tomb until after Peter did, what does Mary's action (verse 11) reveal about her courage?

6. Looking into the tomb, whom does Mary see? How does she explain her tears?

7. Describe Mary's encounter with Jesus. Why, do you think, doesn't she recognize him until he calls her by name?

8. What instructions and information does the Lord give to Mary? What careful distinctions does Jesus make in referring to God, the Father?

9. Compare his instructions to Mary with what Jesus has previously told the disciples in 14:1, 2; 16:10, 28. Why do you think that Mary is the first one to see the risen Lord?

10. Try to put yourself in Mary's place. What are your thoughts and emotions as you go to find the disciples? What do you say when you find them?

John 20:19-23

11. Describe the details of Jesus' meeting with the disciples later that day. What change in atmosphere does his arrival create? How would you illustrate it if you were painting a "before and after" mural of the scene? See also 16:22.

12. How does Jesus convince them that it is truly he, risen from the dead?

13. In commissioning his disciples (verses 21-23), by whose authority and with what power does Jesus send them? To accomplish what purpose? See also Luke 24:45-49. For examples of the fulfillment of these promises, see Acts 8:18-24, 29-38.

John 20:24-31

14. Why do you think that Thomas reacts as he does to the testimony of the other disciples? What would his attitude do to his relationship with the others during the week that follows? What emotions do you experience when you hold out your own opinion against that of a group?

15. What effect does Jesus' reference to Thomas' exact words produce? What things influence Thomas' progress from disbelief to belief? Compare Thomas' response in verse 28 with that of the other disciples (verse 20) and of Mary (verse 16). Why is Thomas' statement so significant?

16. What do you learn in verses 29-31 about *believing?* According to the author, why was this book written? What has been included and what has been left out?

SUMMARY

1. Review the *signs* done by Jesus in this Gospel: 2:1-11; 4:46-54; 5:2-9; 6:1-14, 15-21; 9:1-12; 11:38-47. In what direction do these signs point your thinking about Jesus?

2. In the light of the events described in chapter 20, read 2:18-22. What if the story of Jesus had ended with 19:42? Why is Jesus' resurrection the greatest sign of all?

3. What does Jesus' resurrection mean to you?

AFTERTHOUGHTS

Mary Magdalene, we inherit from you your pattern of seeking to be nearer the Lord Jesus, courage to venture out alone, courage to believe. Thomas, we inherit from you the pattern of testing our faith, of being honest with our doubts and complete in commitment when our doubts are confronted with reality. Let us follow carefully what we learn from both of you!

Discussion 11 / John 21

Catching and Feeding

The true symbol of Christianity is not the cross, but the empty tomb. It is not a dead Christ, but a risen Lord whom the Gospels proclaim. The reality of Jesus' physical resurrection is clearly shown in the incidents John recounts in chapters 20 and 21. The crushing sorrow and fear experienced by the disciples at Jesus' death have been replaced by tremendous joy as they have seen and talked with Jesus, alive from the dead.

In this chapter, two living parables are acted out and discussed—the first, a picture of catching, the second, of feeding. They illustrate the work that Jesus' disciples are intended to perform in the world—to catch followers for Jesus Christ (*I will make you become fishers of men,* Mark 1:17), and to shepherd and feed the new believers in Christ.

John 21:1-14

1. Describe this scene as to time, location (note Mark 14:28), setting, people present, and action. What do you see, hear, smell?

2. What new things are revealed about the risen Lord in this incident? When and where does Jesus appear? What difference does his arrival make?

3. Read aloud the four statements of Jesus recorded in verses 5, 6, 10, 12. What impression do you get? What characterizes Jesus' concern and attitude here?

4. What past experiences might the disciples recall during this breakfast? (Luke 5:1-11; John 6, for example.)

5. Read this conversation aloud as a dialogue. (Peter already has seen Jesus alone since the resurrection—Luke 24:34—when, doubtless, he was forgiven for his denial of the Lord.)

6. When does Jesus initiate this conversation with Peter? What impressions have you had of Peter from his actions thus far in this chapter? Do you ever bound about with helpfulness after you have been reinstated in a relationship?

7. Compare verse 15 with Mark 14:27-29 where Peter makes claim to the degree of his faithfulness above that of his fellow-disciples. (Translators differ on what *these* in 21:15 refers to. "Do you love me more than these others do?" or "Are you more devoted to me than you are to these things?") In either case, what basic question is Jesus putting to Peter?

8. What may be the reason why Jesus asks Simon Peter *three* times if he loves him? (See 18:15-18, 25-27.) Note that Peter denied Christ beside one charcoal fire, while beside another he avows his love and receives his personal commission from the Lord.

9. The connotations of the two Greek words used here for *love* differ. In verses 15, 16 Jesus uses the word for a love involving deliberate choice, while Peter uses the word for a lower form of love involving only personal affection. In verse 17 Jesus uses Peter's word for love. Why might this cause Peter to be grieved?

10. What does Jesus expect Peter to do because he loves him? List the commands Jesus gives Peter. What do these commands mean? What is the motivation for obeying them?

11. What does Jesus teach Peter about what following him will mean for Peter (verses 18-23)?

12. *The disciple whom Jesus loved* (verse 20) is thought to be John, the author of the Gospel. How does Jesus deal with Peter's curiosity about John's future?

13. How should Jesus' repeated command, *Follow me,* help Peter and us to know the direction our lives should take as Christians? What happens when we try to pattern ourselves after other Christians?

14. What rumor does the writer refute in verses 20-23? What future event is clearly expected?

15. Compare verse 25 with 20:30, 31. Why don't we have a complete description of all that Jesus said and did? What are we supposed to do about the information that we do have?

SUMMARY

1. Peter's penitence is indicated by his eagerness to be with the Lord (verse 7), and his desire to obey heartily (verses 10, 11). When we are penitent over our failures, the Lord is as gracious to us as he is to Peter, but the question he asks is the same for each: *Do you love me?* What is your answer to this question?

2. Jesus Christ, who rose from the dead, is alive today. What practical difference will this make to you if you follow Jesus in your home, in your job?

AFTERTHOUGHTS

Fishermen, why were you trying to catch fish when you were called to catch people to follow Jesus? Do we do the same? Is the Lord's advice to you appropriate for us when we do seek to "catch" people? "Try the other side," Jesus said. Reach out to the other side of the street, the other side of town, to people we have not thought would be ready or willing to hear!

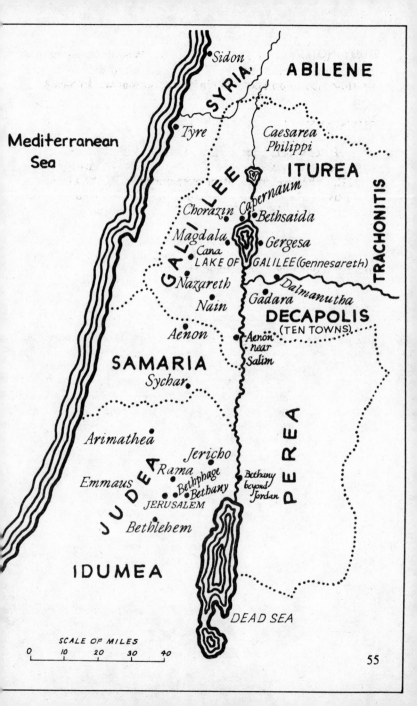

SCALE OF MILES
0   10   20   30   40

How is your prayer life that
like this passage.?

① Glorification =
② help on dependance - unity =
③ prayer for others

Name one person you plan to pray (Jeanette family)

STUDY NOTES

STUDY NOTES

STUDY NOTES

STUDY NOTES

STUDY NOTES

STUDY NOTES